The Roof-Climber's Guide to
TRINITY

Containing a practical description of all routes

By Geoffrey Winthrop-Young

Illustrations by A. M. Mackay

OLEANDER PRESS

The Oleander Press
16 Orchard Street
Cambridge
CB1 1JT

www.oleanderpress.com

First published by W. P. Spalding: 1900
This edition published by The Oleander Press: 2009

© 2009 M. Newbolt, S. Weidlich
All rights reserved.

No part of this publication may be reproduced, stored in a
retrieval system, or transmitted, in any form or by any means
without the prior permission in writing of the publisher, nor be
otherwise circulated in any form of binding or cover other than
in which it is published and without a similar condition including
this condition being imposed on the subsequent purchaser.

A CIP catalogue record for the book is
available from the British Library.

ISBN: 9780906672600

Designed and typeset by Hamish Symington
www.hamishsymington.com

Printed in England

Contents

Introduction 1

Route A: New Court 8

Route B: Cloister Court 14

Route C: Great Court 21

Route D: I Court 30

The Library 39

The Chapel 46

The Great Gate 53

Wayside Problems 56

Appendix One 61

Appendix Two 70

Introduction

"Ille te mecum locus et beatae postulant arces."
— *Horace*

In these athletic days of rapid devolution to the Simian practices of our ancestors, climbing of all kinds is naturally assuming an ever more prominent position. Since the supply of unconquered Alps is limited and the dangers of nature's monumental exercise-ground are yearly increased by the polish of frequent feet and the broken bottles of thirsty souls, aspirants with the true faith at heart have been forced of late years to seek new sensations on the artificial erections of man. Such is the origin of Modern Wall and Roof Climbing. The discovery that these empiric sciences were in reality of enormous antiquity, possessing an extensive history and a literature which includes the greatest verse and prose writers of all ages, has done much latterly to assist their enthusiastic re-development. This branch of the subject is dealt with in the pamphlet *Wall and Roof-climbing*, which contains a short outline of the history and literature, ancient and modern, and an account of the laws, methods, appliances, and phraseology peculiar to the art. The interest shown by many Cambridge residents in the opening up of the new fields, and the vigour with which, in one College at least, the exploration has been prosecuted, gave rise to the idea that a brief Guide to the points best worth attempting with a few suggestions as to the routes most favoured by earlier climbers might be found a convenience. The present leaflet is the result; the precursor we hope, if successful, of similar introductions in other Colleges to regions too long neglected by resident and visitor alike. Doubtless, the fact that a certain bashful conservatism has confined the excursions hitherto to hours of the night has done much to induce this orophismic philistinism, but Alpine ascents suffer under a similar disadvantage, and we confess that, however illogically, we should view with regret an alteration in the College regulations tending to soften the conditions. The darkness, besides comfortably concealing the accumulating soot on hands and person, surrounds the venture with an air of vague mystery, and lends a pleasing uncertainty to the handholds, a depth of impressive gloom to the courts and gutters, and a shadowy outline, fraught with terror, to the colossal-seeming towers, that could be hardly spared; while the recurring step of the night porter, heard when the climber hangs in literal suspense in some awkward lamp-glare, rouses thrills of the chase unknown to legalised stegophilism.

For convenience in description the district has been divided into Routes, and the climber is assumed to be starting from certain definite dormers. These Routes naturally admit of as much variation as do the methods adopted on particular problems, the location of the climber's friends and the length of his reach being the only compulsory limits.

Certain great climbs are separately described and, where occurring in the Route, are referred to in brackets in the text.

Unconventional roads in and out of college are purposely left unmentioned; they are an all too popular abuse of a noble science. Much is here passed briefly over, which in a more exhaustive account could call for longer notice; much also in the College still remains unexplored. The next few years will doubtless see a great advance both in the count of 'possible' climbs and in the methods adopted in negotiating old ones. For ourselves non-residence has closed our period of exploration, but we hand on the work to other feet with full confidence in the powers and numbers of the ever-increasing fraternity who cherish as their motto Browning's lines –

"Though there's doorway behind thee and window before
Go straight at the wall."

Elucidation of Plan

G. GATE: Great Gate
K.E.TOWER: King Edward's Tower
Q.E.TOWER: Queen Elizabeth's Tower
A 'Avenue' Tower
B Turrets
B1 Mutton-hole Corner
C Dormers
D Cat-walls
D1 Kitchen pitch
E Lane Tower
F Iron chimney and supports
G The 'Hole'
H Dip
I Lecture Room Court
J Hostel Chimney
K Exit from Attic window
L Kitchen table
L1 Parade
M Chimney stack
N Sloping parapet
O Ghost turret
P Kitchen ventilator
Q The 'Well'
R 'Newton' Gable and 'Return'
S Bottle-Glass Corner
T Great Chimney
U Tea-table
V Cross gable
XX Chimney Traverse
Y Small chimneys
Z Lodge chimney stacks
β Trinity Lane Corner
θ 16 foot wall
λ 'Tank' Climb
κ I Court Climb

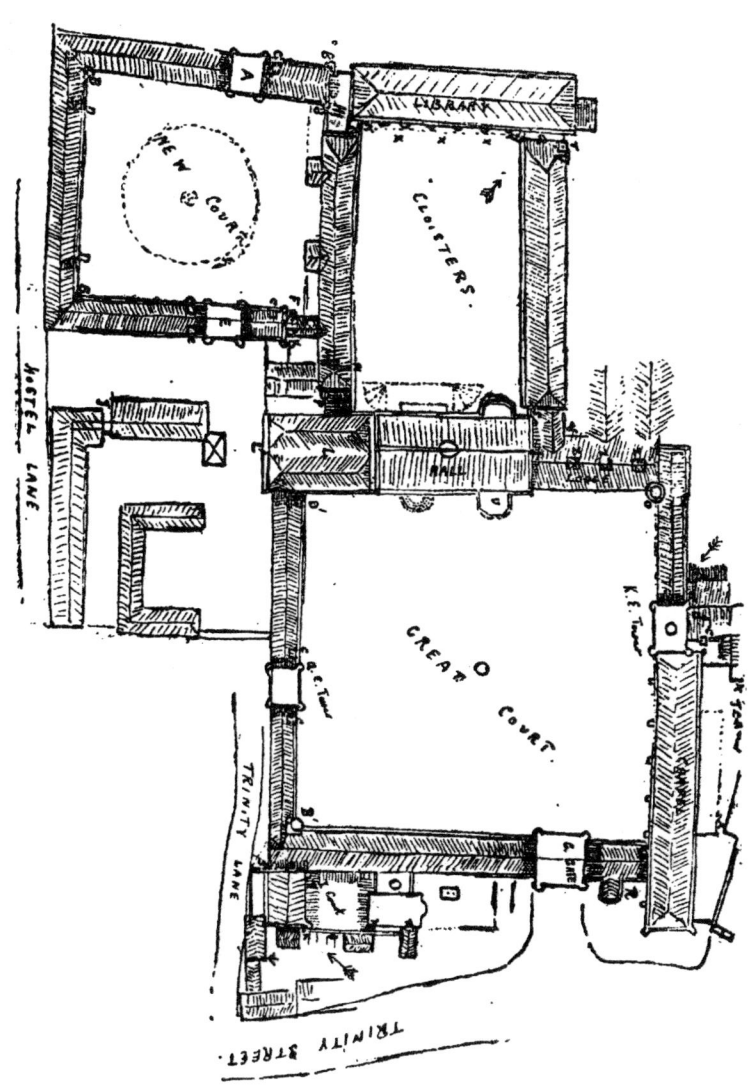

Route A: New Court

*"With tombs and towers and fanes 'twas 'our' delight
To wander in the shadow of the night." – Shelley*

*"Lead, lift at last your soul that walks the air,
Up to the house front, or its back, perhaps –
Whether façade or no, one coquetry
Of coloured brick and carved stone. Stucco? Well,
The daintiness is cheery." – Browning.*

Complete circuit; time 45–60 mins.; guide superfluous, but rope necessary; expense, repair of pipes and possible doctor's fees.

The Tower: The start of our route is made from some window between the 'Avenue' Tower (A) and the 'Dip' (H). The leads can be followed either on the Court or Cam-side until the wall of the Tower is reached. Here the slant roof is ascended over the dormer (C) until near the summit of the gable, when the hand is able to grasp with a stretch the edge of an embrasure above; the help of a small ledge some four feet up being hardly required for the swing up on to the roof. The Turrets here may divert our efforts for a moment; but in deference to the slumbering don it is best to pass rapidly round a convenient ledge on the inside of the crenulations, which removes the necessity of clattering over the roof. The descent is made by the corresponding embrasure on the opposite side, the arms at full length bringing the climber's feet within a few inches of the roof.

Corner Turret: The leads continue on either side. But if the Cam-side route can be taken, the lack of battlements and path on the roof above Garret Hostel Lane compels a return across the gable at the corner, and the climber finds himself at the foot of the Corner Turret, his first 'roof-side problem.' If he be tempted to solve it on his way the only necessary formula (as also for its duplicates B B) is a friendly back-up and the use of the somewhat loose pipe. Care should be taken to avoid touching the summit battlements, as they collapse at a breath.

The little 'Cat-walls' (D D) next present themselves, but no difficulty – except to weak heads; and at the next Corner Turret (B) it is possible either to cross again by the slant-gutters to the Trinity Lane and less comfortable leads, or to follow the ordinary track to the foot of Lane Tower (E).

Lane Tower: This is a more difficult subject than A, and has proved a stumbling-block to many. Ascending over the dormer (C) or close to the wall, it is possible from near the top of the gable for a long reach to get some fingers of the right hand over an embrasure-edge; if the left foot be then raised sufficiently high, a just attainable ledge serves as a foothold – and the rest is mechanical. It is not wise to trust exclusively to the hand, as the cement has twice been known to prove brittle and precipitate a whole party into the gutter.

A friend's shoulder will always solve the difficulty for a short reach. It is safest not to linger here for the view, and the descent is similar to that from Tower A.

Iron-Bar Corner: The next check occurs at the Corner (F), where the joining of the Cloister and New Court is flawed, a steep little piece of narrow tile-roof alone connecting them. If the Lane-side leads have been followed it is comparatively easy to ascend by the stone parapet (K) and descend on to the tile roof. From the other side it is best to cross the dormer (C), step out over the edge and set the left foot on the stanchion which connects the iron-bar chimney (F) with the wall; a long stride carries the right foot across the vasty depths on to the tile-roof dormer (C).

Two alternatives are here again possible. (1) To follow the 'high level' route along the New Court side of the Cloisters roof, over a succession of cross-gables, and past the Turrets (B B) to the Library corner. (2). To cross the Cloister roof and descend on the so-called 'Bicycle-track' which runs round three sides of this Court. The descent of the steep roof can be effected either by the 'chimney stack' (Route B, Plan M), or by the conventional 'gable method', the leader hanging from the top of the tilt by his hands, a second descending him and grasping his ankles, and the rest using the improvised ladder and assisting its subsequent descent. If (2) is followed it is necessary to return at the Library corner either across the roof by the corner-tiles or by climbing down into 'The Hole' (G) and re-ascending to the parapet on the other side.

The Dip: The last and worst difficulty of the circuit has now to be tackled, one which much troubled the early climbers. It is formed by the low block of buildings connecting the corners of the Cloisters and New Courts, and its deep-lying roof is thus overtopped by the higher walls of either. It goes by the name of 'the Dip' (H). The Hole (G) is separated from the Dip (H) by a high crenelated wall which joins the Cloister roof to the Library and forms the narrow 'take off' for the descent. A door in the bottom of this wall, if not locked, may of course be ignored. The first step is apparent, a sloping ledge some four feet below the battlements; but no further steps are forthcoming, and the climber has to perform the delicate task of transferring his hands to his foothold, and thence being lowered or dropping. The crumbling mouldings of an intervening window rather complicate than assist, and if the help of a rope doubled round a pinnacle be not used, the first part will always prove an exciting balance-test for the last to descend. The ascent of the New Court wall, more formidable in appearance, is simplified by the corner turrets. The tallest of the party is placed firmly in the corner formed by either turret with the wall, the leader then scrambles on to his shoulders, head, and finally up-stretched hands, using the rain-pipe as assistance. By the aid of a handhold on a ledge encircling the turret he can now secure a position on the basin-like top of the pipe, and thence reaching up grip the firm parapet ledge and pull up. The last man must depend chiefly on the rope. The pipes are fragile and should be dealt with gently for the sake of future generations. To negotiate the 'Dip' in the opposite direction the same movements are applicable in their reverse order.

Route B: Cloister Court

"Auream quisquis mediocritatem
Diligit, tutus caret obsoleti
Sordibus tecti, caret invidenda
Sobrius Aula." – Horace

"But let my due feet never fail
To walk the studious Cloister's pale,
And love the high-embowed roof
With antique pillars massy proof." – Milton

Complete Circuit; time, 20–40 minutes.

The expedition for our present purpose is assumed to be starting from the New Court and to have just negotiated 'Iron-bar corner' (Plan, F). Direct crossing and descent on to the 'Bicycle Track' by the methods described in Route A are of course possible, but the more usual and sporting path is to follow the top of the tilt towards the Hall, either straddling it or sliding the hands along the top and running the feet simultaneously below along the New Court slope, until the 'chimney-stack' (M) bars further progress.

The Chimney Stack: This can be turned either on the New Court or Hall side. In the former case some awkward reaching is necessary round the chimney sections, with no particular prevention below to a hurried descent on to the kitchen premises; once the chimney is turned it is easy to regain and follow the tilt[1] until a sooty kitchen ventilator and an uncertainty, not as yet cleared up by daylight examination, as to the continuance of the roof advise a return and

---

1   It is possible to gain this point by a most interesting little cross-route from the gyp-room window of a certain famous first-floor Historian. [See Notes, page 61]

an easy descent by the parapet (N). The Hall side is that most usually followed round the chimney stack and calls for a firm grip and a long reach. Holding with the right hand to the summit tiles of the gable and turning the face to the chimney, the left arm must be stretched to its utmost round the stack until the parapet (N) can be reached and grasped, the body and legs the while drifting aimlessly on the steep tiles. It is then not hard to swing around on the left arm and descend by the parapet. This is usually considered a very 'neat' corner.

The Hall: Crossing the corner on to the Hall by a convenient sloping parapet we get our first glimpse of the impressive summits of the Great Court range. The new-comer's attention will, however, be more probably drawn to the nearer heights of the Hall roof, which rises above him in somewhat threatening proximity. A step up on to the creaky wooden path that fringes it and all else is shut out by the impossible slopes of its smooth slates. Time and nerve sufficing an ascent may be attempted, and the slightly raised stone coping which edges either end of the slate-slopes gives the key. Holding its square edges with both hands and placing his feet on the narrow lead gutter, the climber pulls up hand over hand, the tension on the arms keeping the feet from slipping. The stone plaster on the summit is generally embraced with panting satisfaction, as the height makes the strain upon the muscles considerable. A few moments can well be spared to the view, and few could be insensible to its charms. The distant towers of the Great, New and Cloister Courts looming against the dark sky, lit by the flickering lamps far below; the gradations of light and shadow, marked by an occasional moving black speck seemingly in another world; the sheer wall descending into darkness at his side, above which he has been half-suspended on his long ascent; the almost invisible barrier that the battlements from which he started seem to make to his terminating in the Cloisters if his arm slips; all contribute to making this deservedly-esteemed the finest view point in the College Alps[1]. Descent upon the other side is perfectly possible, thus making the traverse of

---

1   [See notes, page 62]

the Hall (Route C, the Hall), but with his circuit in view our climber returns by the path he came, lying on his back, if he be wise, in the gutter, and letting himself down hand after hand by the coping. Either end of the Hall may be ascended, but the poorness and looseness of the coping stones at the kitchen end renders the Lodge edge the only one that can be recommended, more especially for the traverse.

Bottle Glass Corner: Climbing over the parapet at the corner of the Hall (S), a careful step or two along the top of the parapet which unites it at a lower level with that of the Cloister leads again on to the Bicycle Track, passing on the right the walls and corners ornamented with glass and palings by some former Master against the incursions of tourist Dons. It is possible here to clamber a short distance on to the Master's garden side of the Cloister's roof, but lack of path or parapet soon prevents a further advance.

Chimney Corner: The ascent of the Library by the great chimney, whose terrors naturally draw all eyes on reaching the end of the Bicycle Track, is dealt with elsewhere ('The Library'). The configuration of the corner is similar to that in Route A. A deep hole (Q) parts the roof from the Library, but the parapet wall forms a narrow bridge.

Library Traverse: The object now is to complete the fourth side of the circuit by some passage along the Library. A broad ledge (X. X. X.), not conspicuous from below, but running the whole length of the building above the arches, offers from above an obvious route[1]. To gain this it is necessary to cross the parapet close to the Library wall and wriggle down the Chimney (Y) formed by the parapet wall and one of the big projecting columns adorning the face of the Library. A square pipe in the Chimney gives valuable, if uncertain, hand and foothold. The ledge is broad and comfortable, though the protuberant columns would make blindfold

---

1 NB The contiguity of the Vice-Master's rooms calls for a respectful avoidance of all superfluous noise.

walking awkward. A rope is an aid to the nervous. The corresponding Chimney (Y) at the New Court end of the traverse is exactly similar, and once free from its compression a stretch of Bicycle Track completes the circuit.

Route C: Great Court

*"The night has been unruly, where we lay
Our chimnies were blown down, and as they say,
Lamentings heard in the air." – Shakespeare*

*"And I 'eard the brick and the balks rummle down
As the roof gave way." – Tennyson*

Circuit; time, 1–2 hrs. This expedition, offering as it does almost every variety of roof climbing difficulty, and hindered as it is by every form of authoritative residence, has only once been accomplished. In its absolute entirety the circuit has never been completed, the Great Gate forming as yet an unconquered barrier. Sections of it are generally taken in connection with other routes.

Our excursion takes us to the leads on the Lecture-room side of the Great Gate. Avoiding all temptation to stray over the tiles into the almost unexplored back regions of Trinity Street or the problems of I Court (Route D), the first point calling for attention, with the exception of ankle-wringing drain-holes (most difficult to avoid in the dark) is the corner turret (B).

Mutton-Hole Turret: often generously simplified by the College Authorities by means of a species of iron-spoked rope which is left hooked over the battlements. If this is absent, the turret affords excellent practice for 'the men in a tower' method of backing up, and has of course the customary loose pipe. At this corner it is easy again to cross by the lead gutter and join the I Court (Route D, Trinity Lane Corner).

Queen Elizabeth's Tower: On the Great Gate side this Tower is usually too brightly illuminated and porter-swept for elaborate dallying. Its interest is consequently increased. Standing on the roof of the dormer (C) the leader leans against the slates and the others pass over him to the summit of the gable, the last man hanging as ladder for his ascent. A few steps along the edge and the tower is reached, and two embrasures found easily accessible. That on the Great Court side is preferable as the roof-slope towards Trinity Lane is unprotected. On the summit of the Tower a few moments may be spent on the corner turrets which offer little resistance. The embrasures on the opposite side, a little caution and the human ladder, make descent easy on to the dormer (C) and the leads are regained.

Kitchen Pitch: The steep wall with which the Kitchen buildings mark their superiority to the ordinary dwelling-room roofs looks from below a serious obstacle (D). Hesitation is here again inadvisable in the unfriendly lamp glare. It is possible to climb from the roof of the ever-present dormer (C) with something of a spring to the projecting cornice on the Kitchen building wall, which terminates some little distance above on the right and overhangs the Court. A more rapid and safer method is to use the strong man's shoulders from his position on dormer C. The edge of the roof can then be reached, and the last man pulled up by his wrists as he jumps. If he is terror-stricken you may swing him out over space.

The Kitchen Roof: This is rambling and less clearly defined, some little time may well be spent in roaming over its easy angles. It is customary after surmounting the Kitchen Pitch (D) to turn over to the left either by the gently sloping gutters or directly up the edge of the cross gable and descend on the 'parade' (L1), a delightful parapeted plateau which overlooks the Hostel and 'lends broad verge' to Lane Tower. Return can be made from its New Court end over small tilts on to the 'Kitchen Table' (L), a flat stretch between the main gables of the roof, whence a small ladder leads on to the wooden path encircling the Hall.

The Hall: A slightly higher step than that necessary on the opposite side (Route B) and the highest pinnacle of the many which fringe the Hall battlements blocks the view on the right. Their excrescences make all these pinnacles easy of ascent to steady heads, but cement ornamentation is never too trustworthy. Passing the 'Tea Place' (U), where tradition relates a night party was once entertained by an early climber, the high and unnegotiable wall which terminates the Hall is found to make a direct descent onto the Lodge impossible, without, of course, unsportsmanlike 'fixed' ropes. The quickest route is no doubt to return and pass round the Hall along the path traversed in Route B, but the true 'inside edge' of the circuit is better followed by making the traverse of the Hall (Route B, the Hall) at its Lodge end, finishing at Bottle-glass Corner (Route B, Plan S).

The Lodge: A natural awe, combined with apparent difficulties, has done much to prevent this part of the circuit being often visited; in fact it is only known to have been crossed once[1] on an expedition referred to later

---

1 Since repeated, without rope.

(The Chapel). A cross-gable (V) connects the Cloister roofs with the Lodge, but at a lower level. Access to this cross-gable is barred by a high wooden paling. Arrived, therefore, at 'Bottle-glass Corner' it is necessary to clamber round the railing and back along its other side, clinging to the perpendicular wooden slats until it is possible to drop on to the cross-gable. Alternative routes are here again to the fore: (1) To cross the House roof and pass boldly along the leads in front of the top storey windows; (2) To continue along the summit of the gable with its two blocking chimney stacks. The latter is the less nervous, if more severe route. On the occasion of its first crossing the climber provided himself with a rope weighted at the end. This was quickly swung round the stacks as they presented themselves, grasped and used as a most necessary support in the task of circumvention. The last of these being conquered the corner behind the 'Ghost' turret (O) gives easy access to the broad and soul-refreshing plains of the 'Munro' roofs, where a short interval of reposeful contemplation of the Master's garden and the Bowling-green should be taken to recover from the late nervous hurry, and recruit forces for the grim-looking wall of King Edward's Tower.

King Edward's Tower: The difficulty of the Chapel-climb and the many assaults made at various times upon it from different points give it a history of its own only inferior to that of the Library chimney or the Aiguille Dru. This and the fact that, like the Library, its highest point is attainable from the actual ground without the usual assistance of a friend's attic window, endow it with a separate entity, which it is hoped may justify its treatment in a distinct section (The Chapel). As the ascent of King Edward's Tower forms the final and most important portion of this description, to avoid repetition it is assumed that the leader has performed the necessary contortions and the last man enacted his pendulum trick and that the roof of the tower has been reached.

The Chapel: Scraping round the belfry an almost unnoticed step places the broad wooden paths and mild slopes of the Chapel roof beneath the victorious feet of the climbers, who will have earned the delights of the view which bursts upon them – the long vista of half-seen spires, the shadowy courts, and the bright lamps of traffic on Trinity Street – looked down upon from these seemingly immeasurable heights, find their only parallel, to our mind, in the Zermatt lights viewed at night from the Matterhorn or Wasdale Head from the Great Gable. The descent from the Chapel on to the 'Newton' roof is somewhat similar to that of the Cloisters side of the Dip (Route A, Plan H); the difference being that whereas in the latter task a flat plain awaited the climber, here the summit of a steep gable, indifferently protected on the Trinity Street side, is his prospective landing-place some 12 feet lower. A ledge four feet below the battlements forms the only break, where the neat balance manoeuvre of bringing the hands to the foothold, as in the Dip, has to be accomplished under more trying circumstances, and the climber steadied by the rope or by the hands of friends below on to the narrow edge; for the last man without the friendly rope this is again an interesting moment, as it is impossible for his companions to secure any firm position from which to assist him. A minute more would bring our expedition back to its starting point, were it not that the formidable walls of the Great Gate forbid all further progress. If, however, more exercise is desired, futile efforts may be made upon its pipes (The Great Gate) or a few moments spent in rambling out over the little 'Return' (R) commanding Trinity Street. Its final stone gable point is loose and should not be trusted unless a more hurried termination is desired than the customary staircase[1].

---

1 [See notes, page 62]

Route D: I Court

"When they were all on an hepe,
The behind gonne uplepe,
And clamber up on others faste
And up his nose on hyen caste
And trodden faste on others' heides
And stampe." – Chaucer

"Upon the masonry unseen,
Secure and swift, from "shore" to "shore,"
With silent footfall travelling o'er." – Clough.

These roofs are little known, and a good deal has yet to be done in the way of thorough exploration. The irregularity of its outline has hitherto prevented the accomplishment of the complete circuit, and the account here given is more of the nature of notes on individual pioneer climbs than directions to a general Route. These climbs were originally undertaken with a view to finding some ascent from ground to roof without the use of the customary window; the only other two known being unpopular – the Library traverse chimney ('The Library') on account of its severity and the Chapel ascent by reason of its early locked gate ('The Chapel').

Passing into the I Court we have on two sides the high lecture room building and behind us the Great Court roofs, the fourth side is blocked by a 16 foot wall which defies direct attack.

Tank Chimney: The most promising point is the 'Tank Chimney' (λ) formed in the left-hand corner by the wall, the buildings and a short connecting wall. A 'back and knee' up this offers three alternatives. (1) To fall into the tank on the other side of the connecting wall, an easy passage in the dark. (2) To crawl along the wall (θ) towards Trinity Lane. (3) To follow its continuation (β) in the opposite direction on the chance of finding some assailable point in the great walls above us. The second alternative may be almost at once rejected – a low roof projecting over its sloping summit, and further on a protuberant chimney make its passage a hazardous enterprise. If the third be followed, the wall, skirting the 'tank', continues at irregular levels with the high buildings on the immediate left and the back gardens on the right, until it is cut at right angles by a steep gable roof. Surmounting a 12 foot wall the ascent of the loose tiles, no easy matter, still leaves a height of wall (π) on the left, whose ascent must be always unsafe, if not impossible, without 'artificial aids' from above[1]. There is nothing but to return or roam along the garden walls.

'I Court' Climb: The uncompromising-looking right angle (κ) between the Turret (δ) and the wall (θ) in the opposite corner is the true, though difficult, line of attack.

---

1 [See notes, page 62]

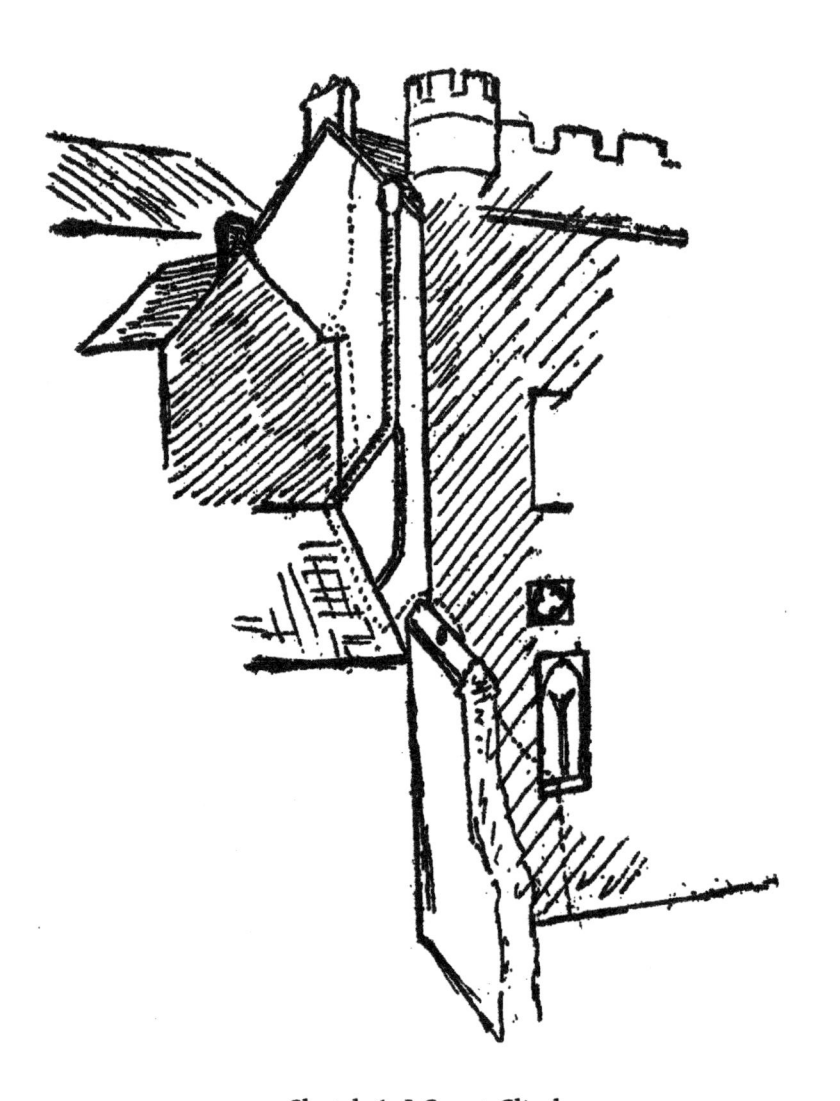

Sketch 1: I Court Climb
Pitches: 1st, 16ft; 2nd, 8ft; 3rd, 11ft.

First Pitch: The 'tallest of the party' is used as a staircase, and from his head the leader is able to get a hold for his right hand in the little slit-window of the Turret. By this he can support himself while his supporter substitutes his hands for his head and thrusts him another two feet up the corner. The visible top of the wall can now be reached, but a slanting coping refuses all hold to the groping left hand until it tries the exact point where the wall joins the Turret. Here the coping is cut away to allow for a pipe-trap and gives a first-class hold. The right hand joins the left, and a kick down against the rough wall yields a much-needed relief to the supporter.

Second Pitch: Passing round behind the turret up a little slate roof, the end wall of a gable is encountered, which runs parallel to the main building and is joined to it by a broad gutter. The eight foot corner between the two buildings is mounted by the aid of a slanting pipe and the gutter edge. (See Sketch 1.)

Third Pitch: The final roof is now close above us, but the surmounting steep wall is too high for one to reach, and the gutter too narrow to allow of two piling up. The method best adopted is for one climber to place his feet as far up as convenient on the opposing gable, and with shoulders leant against the main wall to bridge the gulf. The second climber stepping to his knee, his shoulder, and then pulling up.

Trinity Street View-point: From the roof now reached, an excursion is often made, more interesting from the surprise generally produced by the discovery of its existence, than from any climbing merit. This is to reach the roofs of Trinity Street from the College. A step from the Trinity Lane corner of the I Court roof takes us into the adjoining slates of a long building (Y), whose roof as we pass along its gable-edge slopes down unprotected towards Trinity Lane and the back yards. A firm connection crossed, another flat roof is traversed by its wall-edging to an open plateau where a lofty tile-gable rises before us. Ascending this by the aid of a dormer, no Cortes could be more surprised than is the average explorer to find the splendours of Trinity Street spread at his feet. As it is only a one-time sensation, and the roofs crossed are private, climbers can well afford to be forbearing in its enjoyment.

Brick Turret: At the corner opposite to the point where the 'I Court climb' emerges on the roof stands a brick turret (γ). This can be as easily surmounted by the narrow chimney between the adjacent chimney-stack and its walls. From its summit we look down upon the parallel-running roof of the Great Court, whose eaves are merged in the ten-foot wall descending from the higher I Court roofs.

Trinity Lane Corner: To reach the Great Court roofs the easiest way is to cross the slates from the foot of the Brick Turret (γ) or to traverse along the foot of the chimney-stack (E) and lower oneself carefully on to the coping edge of the roofs below from the down-slanting end of the ten-foot wall. The iron palings of Trinity Lane immediately below give the necessary interest.

From here it is easy to clamber round a chimney-stack (x) and descend by a corner gutter to Muttonhole turret (Route C, Mutton-hole Turret).

Round Chimney Stack: Following the circuit, the Great Court roof is kept to until the junction of the second side of the I Court Square declares itself on the right by its (slightly lower) brick wall. This is surmountable at various points; perhaps the most interesting is the balance round the Round Chimney-stack (L) reached from a Great Court dormer roof. Two uninteresting and large flat roofs succeed, one remarkable for a large glass cupola, and the second separated by a high parapet from the first.

From the end[1] building the difficulties of an ascent from the first attempted wall route ('Tank Chimney' 2nd alternative), which must be overcome if ever an I Court 'complete circuit' is to be achieved, are more apparent; and an excellent view is obtained of 'The Wilderness' (Route C start), the name given to the jungle of steep tiled roofs which fills the space between I Court, the Great Court, and Trinity Street. One attempt made

---

1 [See notes, page 62]

upon them from the Great Court gable was swiftly abandoned, and their old unprotected tile gables and possible disconnections are still unexplored ground.

The Library

"Ne can I tell, ne can I stay to tell
This part's great workmanship and wondrous power,
That all this other world's work doth excel,
And likest is unto that Heavenly tower
That Jove hath built for his own blessed bower." – Spenser

"– The blind walls
Were full of chinks and holes, and overhead
Fantastic gables, crowding, stared" – Tennyson

The Library: A certain halo of mystery and myth which surrounds the Library makes its ascent the most cherished project of the youngest roof-climber, while its inherent climbing properties win for it from the oldest the place of first importance among Trinity ascents. The variety of ways by which it is traditionally supposed to have been climbed is only equalled by the notability of those, from Byron downwards, to whom ascents are attributed. Hardly a college generation passes without its decorated statues or legend of a pipe ascent 'vouched for by the porter.' Reduced to hard facts the majority of these (concerning which anything is discoverable) prove to have been either accomplished on chance-found ladders, or up the turret stairs, breaking in at the window below and out at the door above. It has been rumoured lately that the Council, in view of one of the most recent 'ladder' ascents, contemplates moving the great chimney or in some way blocking it. We should beg respectfully to deprecate this. The precaution of not leaving ladders about would meet the same end. Anyone who has ever seen the great chimney climb from the St John's Backs will agree that the sort of person who can fairly master its difficulties will be the last to do any injury through carelessness or malice to the Library itself.

The Library Traverse Chimney: The ordinary method of approaching the Great Chimney is by the Cloister roof bicycle track, but those desirous of making the complete ascent from the ground can start from the corner of the grass plot in the Court below, and force their way up the narrow corner chimney with the aid of the pipe[1] until the overhanging cornice of the traverse (Route B, Library Traverse) stops progress; the swing out and pull up over this is a considerable effort. From the traverse the Great Chimney is gained by the corner climb (Plan Y) before described.

The Great Chimney: Where the Cloisters roof joins the Library the tiled gable slopes steeply down some twelve feet (forming 'the Well' Plan Q). The end of the slope is connected with the Library wall by a gutter. At the

---

1 The continuation of this square pipe is one of the traditional ascents. The attempt is not advised for sane persons. The corresponding Library traverse chimney at the other corner is also climbable.

outside end of this, overhanging the Master's garden, rises the chimney stack; its inside wall distant some 3½ feet from the Library, its front some two feet broad and its length running four feet back into the tiled gable. Nine feet above the gutter a narrow ledge runs round the stack, and nine feet higher the stack walls set back, leaving a broad sloping ledge; slightly lower than this and some feet out to the left is the sill of a blind window in the Library wall opposite. Eleven feet above the sill projects a big cornice, with only a narrow crack between its edge and the stack. Above this is a high parapet. The whole 'chimney' has been climbed 'back and knee' throughout, but the less exhausting method for the ordinary climber is first to ascend up the roof gable to the point where it joins the chimney. Here the second man can anchor safely with the rope. Traversing back along the narrow ledge, a small hold for his left foot in the Library wall will help the said climber to fix himself across the chimney with his shoulders against the stack; a wriggle or two of the conventional 'back and knee' type and he can get his left hand on to the sloping ledge; placing his right against the opposite wall and

Sketch 2: Great Chimney Climb on the Library.
Height: 31ft.

supporting himself on his arms he swings across out of the chimney on to the sill of the blind window, standing, for it is awkward to get up from a sitting position. A short breathing space and he leans out again, this time with his right hand on the sloping ledge, and bridges his body again across the chimney. This is the most thrilling point, for he looks down upon the depths of the garden between his knees. A moment or two's hand-shoving and shoulder-scraping follows, and then the hands can reach the edge of the cornice and the body be drawn up through the crack. The high parapet is then readily surmounted and the roof gained. The consequent blissful period of statue-salutation and the reposeful contemplations of the quiet 'Backs' with the reflected stars twinkling up from the unseen Cam can only be appreciated by those who have overwon the muscular obstacles of the ascent, magnified by the shadows and the tension of darkness. The descent is comparatively simple. The climber lowers himself by his arms from the cornice, and jamming for a moment across the chimney can shift his right hand to a small ledge which projects just below the former and drop his feet to the sloping ledge. The rest is a quick 'back and knee' scrape downward. A descent has been made at the opposite end of the Library into the 'Hole' (Plan G), but it was made more upon the rope than the wall.

An unseen iron ladder at the end of the gutter at the foot of the Great Chimney leads down upon the low roofs adjoining the Library Annexe, but opens the way to nothing worthy of attention[1].

---

1   See notes, p63.

The Chapel

"Now walk the angels on the walls of heaven." – Marlow

"– Heroes tall,
"Dislodging pinnacle and parapet." – Tennyson

Unlike the Library, the Chapel has no romance of history or tradition. To certain knowledge it has only been ascended once, and that, quite recently. Something of this neglect is no doubt due to the fact that before the route from the foot of King Edward's Tower was laboriously worked out, the Master's Lodge proved an effective bar to any assault upon its only apparently accessible side. Now that the road is known and that, with the Library and the I Court climb, it enjoys the distinction of a separate entity, the unquestionable interest and length of its ascent should win for it the attention it deserves.

Passing under King Edward's Tower and through the iron gate towards the Junior Common Room (this gate is locked early, and necessitates the climb being undertaken at an early evening hour), various ways are possible to attain our present object – the main roof, which separates us from the Bowling Green. We can ascend by the door we are passing, over the skylight and up a steep corner, or pull up by a big gutter from the Junior Common Room steps or by many other obvious corners.

The High Level Route: The best and most various start is the 'chimney' formed by the farthest corner of the Chapel Vestry and the low building on the opposite side of the passage abutting on the wall of St John's Lane. Once on the roof of this building we pass along its inside edge behind the back windows of the Junior Common Room until a steep corner on our left, simplified by a broad shelf and a strong lead gutter above, brings us out between two of the multitude of small gables which here recall the lower Alps that usually form the approach to some famous peak. A passage along the gutter over a gable or two, and a drop down on to the edge of another, and the tiles of the main roof are reached. This lofty gable runs out from King Edward's Tower at right angles to the Chapel, and since the latter projects on this side some thirty feet beyond the Tower a deep corner is formed into which the slope of the tilt fits (see Sketch 3). Many attempts were made to find a path to the summit from this roomy base. The great chimney-stack which rises from the roof opposite the outside corner of the Chapel offered a possible 'chimney', but the breadth of the gap and the fact that the feet had to be stayed against the sharp wall corner made the ascent of the great height a dangerous venture at best. A blind arch in the brick wall of the Chapel, nearer towards the Tower, combined with a sloping ledge high up in the actual corner, was also attempted, but after a 'foot and stretched arm' chimney ascent of the shallow arch it was found impossible to reach the ledge, and even if gained, doubtful whether further progress were assured. A similar failure was an attempt to traverse out from the top of the gable along the old bricks of King Edward's Tower and gain the same ledge by means of a rain-pipe.

Sketch 3: Chapel Climb (King Edward's Tower)

The Chapel Corner: No alternative was or is left but the Lodge face of the tower. To gain the foot of this we climb to the gable edge round the back of the big stack and shuffle along it until it merges in the wall. Some three feet to the right the tower ends and the stone coping of the 'Munro' buildings begins, its upper edge about on a level with our faces. The roof below on the right slants abruptly down to the Bowling Green, and a fixed wire crossing the gable diagonally two feet above its top elaborates the process of balancing upon it. Bending under this wire and using the hook to which it is fastened as a hold for the left hand, the right is reached out and up (with the wire pressing on the spine), until it can grip the stone edge, the left joins it, and an upward sideways jump and pull finishes the corner.

King Edward's Wall: The circuit of the Great Court (Route C) has now been joined and the problem reached so lightly skipped over on that excursion. The high plastered wall looks hopeless enough, but a couple of rainpipes and windows give promise of some help. Many failures attended the first attempts of the first party;

ultimate success was achieved by the following method: The 'tallest of the party', supported by a second, establishes himself close to the wall on the left slope of the slight rise in the centre of the flat roof. From his shoulders the leader can get a crumbly right hand hold on the over-mouldings of the little window, and with his left hand on the rain pipe and his left foot fixed against it maintain himself for the customary substitution of hands for supporting shoulders. Inch by inch he is shoved up the wall depending largely on his left hand, for the thrust from below has become diagonal owing to his crossing towards the pipe and the necessity of the supporters keeping to the central gable in order to reach his feet at all. Balance is now a matter of consideration; the right hand is raised slowly and at last can just reach the edge of the embrasure slightly to the left above; burning his boats behind him the climber swings loose on his arm, brings his left to join it, and with a kick down at the smooth pipe is over the edge[1].

Descent can be made by the Great Gate end (Route C, Chapel). A number of small scrambles may be had over

---

1 [See notes, page 63]

the forest of irregular gables in the neighbourhood of the Junior Common Room; the most fertile in result is the passage reached from any of these buildings along the wall of St John's Lane to the archway opening on to the street; this can be easily surmounted by its ivied projections, and a spring upward lays the whole new world of the St John's College roofs at some future explorer's feet. On the occasion before alluded to (Route C, the Lodge) of the crossing of the Lodge, the solitary rambler, leaving the farthest corner of New Court at noon, traversed unnoticed the New Court, Cloisters, Hall, and Lodge, and descending by the 'Chapel Corner' passed along the Lane wall, over the gate and finished on the St John's roofs. This is the longest excursion in direct distance possible in Trinity. Future generations with nothing 'New' left to attempt in their own precincts may well keep in mind the advice in 'Sordello',

"– Let us scale this tall,

Huge foursquare line of red brick…

– Scale the roof

Of solid tops and o'er the slope you slide."

The Great Gate

*"At times the spires and turrets half-way down
Pricked through the mist; at times the great gate shone
Only;" – Tennyson's Gareth and Lynette[1]*

*"Until we came unto the city wall
And the Great Gate; then, none knew whence or why,
Disquiet on the multitudes did fall." – Shelley*

The Tower of the Great Gate with its disquieting precipices put an abrupt termination to our Route C. It remains and is not unlikely to remain – with all caution

---

1   [See notes, page 64]

we say it – the one unclimbed summit in Trinity. The only possible points of assault are the corner behind the projecting Court Turret on the 'Newton' roof and the corresponding corner on the I Court side. In either case an old iron pipe running straight up the wall one foot from the corner and passing through a small cornice just before reaching the battlements forms the narrow way. That on the 'Newton' side is the most often attempted; the corner is deeper and better screened; the Turret wall approaches nearer and offers possible rests upon a ledge some third of the height, and on a back-sloped corner near the summit; the pipe itself also stands further out from the wall, allowing good grip for the hands behind. Thus grasped and with the feet thrust against the worn bricks the pipe is walked up hand over hand, the joint fastenings giving occasional standing-place for the feet. There are five of these joints with five feet of pipe between each. A patch of concrete in the wall between the third and fourth interferes with the free passage of the hands. The strain upon the arms is naturally considerable, and the height making a slip undesirable, the method is often adopted of threading a rope held from below back and forwards through the pipe-to-wall fastenings during the ascent. The cornice, coming at the point where the climber is most exhausted, has never yet been surmounted. A rope lowered from above would give protection for its attempt, but deprive it of the credit of a 'fair' climb. The pipe on the I Court side is considerably shortened by an aspiring little bit of the Great Court roof, but it is set closer to the wall, has no assistance from the Turret ledges, and feels, if anything, more rheumatic in its joints than its somewhat nervous neighbour. A proposal to throw over a ball with attendant string and rope from one side of the Tower to the other is perhaps fantastic; and is it fair?

Wayside Problems

"Ὦ μοι γένοιτ ἀν αἰθέρος θρονος" – *Aeschylus*

*"Ich bin herunter gekommen
Und weiss doch selber nicht wie."* – *Goethe*

Innumerable small wall-scrambles offer themselves in every corner of the College, A few examples are here mentioned.

The Cloisters: First in order of age, for it is one of the many Freshman's worshipping places, stands the Library Pillar, the corner column of the Cloister Court arches at the New Court end of the Library. The exacting, if not hazardous feat is to make the circuit of the block on the ledge encircling it a foot above the ground, a nice balance and the use of the 'fall-slowly-and-catch' grip can accomplish it in under a minute, but fruitless hours are as often the result[1].

'Chimney' climbs can be had between many of the columns of the Cloister arches, and excursionists are not seldom rescued by ladders from the cornices that run round the Court at the level of the higher windows; the precaution of a rope slung from window to window avoids this ignominious end to a somewhat pointless attempt.

The summit of the harmonising gazebo on this side of the Hall has not yet been reached; the 'chimney' between the side pilasters, or the ledges by the Hall door, offer a possible means.

The first floor windows and ledge of the Court can be reached by the balustrade and pipe opposite the Buttery windows.

---

1   [See notes, page 64]

New Court: Not much is to be found here. The lower roofs on either side of the entrance to the Cloisters suggest themselves as possible steps to higher things. The creepers are best left alone in spite of Bishop Heber's general maxim, 'To creep beneath the tower and climb the ivy tree'.

The Hostel: Certain first floor windows of New Court can be entered from the Hostel side by means of the pipe in the kitchen side of 'Lane' Tower and the low kitchen roofs. In the space between the wing of the Garret Hostel buildings nearest to New Court and the main building a fine brick chimney is formed (J), having for its upper exit, if desirable, the small staircase window on the upper floor of E staircase. Something has yet to be done on the kitchen roofs opposite to these buildings.

Great Court: On the Hall side of Queen Elizabeth's Tower, between the turret and the wall a way has been made to the first floor windows; this, possibly, may be continued to the roof. Many of the windows are negotiable by the pipes and projecting over-ledges.

The Chapel porch is a tempting though porter-swept goal.

The corner behind the 'Ghost' turret (Plan O) might be converted into a shorter road to the Chapel climb; it has only been half ascended.

The Hall porch is a famous test of style. Either pillar and the disused lamp hooks are the basis for the exhibition.

As before stated ('The Chapel') there are many good exercise scrambles to be found in the neighbourhood of the Junior Common Room. From the roof of the Chapel vestry a certain height may be reached up the 'chimneys' formed by the buttresses.

Whewell's Court: This has received no attention among the Routes, the nature of its roofs precluding all possibility of safe progress. Some scrambles, however, may be found on its walls; notably in the 'billiard table' Court, the ascent to the upper windows by the corner on the grass plot side of the Sidney Street gate (in which a ladder is usually hanging), and the 'chimneys', blocked by ledges, between the lately-built window projections.

The adventurous reader has now been conducted up, down, or along all the roofs best worth visiting in our district, and the termination of the Expeditions gives him the desired opportunity of retiring and washing off the sooty illusions. The Guide begs permission to do likewise. An expert will, doubtless, find many faults in it, both of commission and omission, to criticise and improve upon, but its existence will have been justified if it has succeeded in providing the young stegophilist making his first night venture upon the Trinity Roofs, with a clue, however poor, to the creditable unravelling of their somewhat complex mazes.

"Inde pedum sospes multa cum laude reflexit,
Errabunda regens tenui vestigia filo;
Ne labyrintheis e flexibus egredientem
Tecti frustraretur inobservabilis error." – Catullus

Appendix One

Handwritten notes transcribed from Geoffrey Winthrop-Young's personal copy of the Guide, now housed in the Wren Library, Trinity College, Cambridge.

Page notes

p15: This note applied to Lord Acton. It became the joke against our contemporary R. V. Laurence, himself also a noted historian, that on Acton's death, he moved into those rooms in order that this note should be taken as applying to him.

p7: The view from the Hall. This passage received the compliment of being included in Sydney Waterhouse's Anthology of Great Passages, *In Praise of Cambridge* (entered there as by 'Anon')

p29: View from the Chapel. This passage is quoted at length in *On Foot*, an anthology by Hugh MacDonald, 1942. (Oxford University Press).

p32: The descent of this slope must be always impossible without a rope, and darkness has hitherto preventing ascertaining how far below the edge of the roof the wall joins. Return must be made by the shallow chimney, before traversed, to the right of the chimney-stack, or with a friendly shoulder and a 'pull up' on the firm coping on the left.

p37: It is possible to descend from the end building immediately to the left of the large chimney-stack onto the top of the left gable of the double roof below. The descent is facilitated by a shallow 'chimney' in the wall, with a pipe in its corner. A lead gutter ledge makes good a handhold on the right on the descent of the steep gable tiles into the flat bottom on the right, between the two ridges. At some distance to the left this roof is cut at right angles by a steep tile ridge. Turning along the summit of this, to the right, further progress is barred by a chimney-stack, and a few feet beyond by the high wall of a projection wing from Trinity Street, crossing at right angles. This looks impossible, and would be risky to attempt from the unprotected and high pitched roof. Returning to the flat depression, it is easy to reach the top of the second gable, and from here, if ever, the 'I Court Circuit' must be completed, as the wall from the 'Tank Chimney' abuts some way below the edge of the steeply pitched tiles

p45: The Master told my father that his 'two small sons' had been found up on this, after reading this guide. One is Sir Nevile Butler, the diplomat; the other, Jim Montague Butler, the Vice-Master (1951).

p51: Since done with only two men.

[p53: Handwritten addition by GWY.]

p57: Library Pillar. I found this circuit in my first term, ragging with Felix Levi after Hall. I jumped the flight of steps up to Hall on the same evening – all but one step. Whewell jumped the whole flight, in cap and gown, as my father reported seeing.

First Edition

The guide was produced as a May Week joke like *Horace at Athens* in a former generation. Hence the hurried proof-correcting etc.

Sandy Mackay and Hilton in the Long Vac Term checked my text, as it came from Jena. Hilton developed an attachment for the crossing into John's by the then ivy-covered arch. They repeated it three times, after midnight, returning each time by the Trinity Gate entrance. Naturally, the Porter remarked three entries and no exit! Inquiries – and they were sent down for the Long. (So commenced two climbs to the peerage.)

In the Autumn, 1901, the Vice-Master, Aldis Wright, declared that the College Council must take cognisance of roof-climbing, and decide whether or not it should be declared illegal. The Council appointed George Trevelyan and Gilbert Walker (later Hydrographer Royal in India) as a Committee of Inquiry, with power to co-opt me as non-resident member. It was quite fun. We climbed everything in full daylight, with two of the Porters carrying the fire-ropes behind us in procession! As a result of the report, the sport was made – officially – illegal.

Earlier climbing: I searched hard for records. Edward Bowen used to climb on the Chapel roof; but he got there up turret stairs. The same was done by Dr Roger Wakefield, father of Ted and Cuthbert who later climbed with me. Byron, when he 'decorated the Library statues', got there by breaking in to the turret stairs to the roof.

The Roof-Climber's Guide to St John's: produced in imitation of the first edition, by a post-war group consisting largely of Johnsian Blues. Hartley (thrice stroke of the VIII), Oliver Grag (who'd been under me in Italy), Darlington (another doctor) etc. They invited me to attend a solemn meet and showed me the climbs and told me they'd copied the Trinity Guide's style as close as might be!

The Great Gate: first climbed by Horace de Vere Cole: the practical joker and athlete, who also climbed with me. Hartley climbed it on the street side after the war for the first time.

The Hall: when I first took Clague up this (the 3rd ascent) he tied his hanky to the pilaster on top – tearing off the corner with his name. St John Parry, our tutor, had specimens of all hankies in college brought, identified Claque's, and was so pleased at being able to spring his detective cleverness on us, that he forgot even to gate us!

Early Climbers
Sandy Mackay: Became a judge, and Lord Mackay. He also played tennis for Scotland, etc., and climbed in the Alps with me in early years. Broke his leg with me in Aran.

F. Dobson: Became Professor of Greek at Bristol University. A big powerful fellow, fond of me, and a useful 'second'.

C. Clague: Climbed with me in the Alps, Wales etc. Put his knee out playing chess! A good athlete and swimmer. Became later HM Inspector with my help.

George M. Trevelyan

A. Wedgwood: Odd adventurous fellow. Later in S. America. Wrote one good novel. Married Longstaff's sister; died in war. Brother of Colonel Josh W. and Sir Ralph W. Insisted, when I took him up the Library, on carrying four green paper parasols for the four statues. Fonder of me than I of him I think, as he had a red-haired man's temper!

W.W. Greg: Later the famous Elizabethan scholar and writer. A keen climber when young.

John Talbot: Didn't climb, but always entertained us in his attic in New Court, and spied us from his window. Later Headmaster of Haileybury.

Second Edition

This was a tragedy. With the strong survival of climbing at Cambridge after the war, roof-climbing also became a vogue. The *Guide* was out of date. And one Hurst, a son of Sir Cecil Hurst, legal adviser at the League, a minor member of the group, got my leave to re-issue it.

He sent me his 'additions', and I took trouble to re-write them in the original style, and arrange the new issue generally.

Suddenly he sent me his final proofs, *after* his last revision, saying it had gone to press. I found that – from some young man's vanity? – and a complete disregard of propriety and my rights – he had coolly scrapped *all* my writing and arrangement, omitted what he pleased, *stirred* my text about, put in his own second-rate jokes, and even muddled up my quotations – not seeing apparently, that half their point lay in their juxta-positions!

I telegraphed at once to stop publication. Result, an interview with him, all but in tears – his 'one literary venture' and so on. Of course, I had to let it go, rather than hurt his pocket and his vanity too much.

But it remains a silly hotch-potch.

Appendix Two

[A 1948 typed note found in Sir Richard Glazebrook's copy of the *The Roof-Climber's Guide to Trinity* – recorded by R. Lawford, Honorary Librarian, Alpine Club, London. August 1986.]

This copy belonged to Professor Norman Collie F.R.S., scientist, artist and sometime President of the Alpine Club. I gave it to him on its appearance in 1900 and it returned to me after his death in 1945.

It was written as a May Week joke, to appear during the festival days at Cambridge at the end of the summer Term; as were its famous predecessors, *Horace at Athens* etc., by Sir George Otto Trevelyan.

I wrote it from memory while I was studying at Jena, and sent back the MS to my friend and climbing colleague A. M. Mackay, Scholar of Trinity College, for him to check the accounts. He drew the illustrations but did not alter the text. Mackay afterwards became Lord Mackay of the Scottish bench.

Mackay, verifying the accounts, took with him my brother E. Hilton Young (afterwards Lord Kennet of the Dene) on the midnight climbs. Hilton was so fascinated by the beauty of the traverse over the ivy-clad arch into St John's College, that he crossed it three times, outward, returning each time by the (then) locked Trinity Gate. The Porters naturally remarked upon three successive entrances after twelve, with no exit. Inquiries followed and both distinguished men were 'sent down' for the Long Vac (not a severe penalty). Thus began two ascents to the peerage.

In my absence the proofs were poorly corrected; but the joke was popular and the edition soon disappeared.

Earlier Climbing

After long research, I could find no authentic evidence of climbing on the College roofs. Excursions out of windows on to the leads must, of course, have been popular for centuries.

Edward Bowen, the great Harrow master, got on to Chapel; but I found he broke out of Turret stairs.

Byron got on to the Library roof, and decorated the statues; but I found, again, that he had broken in at the door of the winding staircase and out at the top on to the roof.

My explorations were between 1895 and 1899. I took with me at different times – F. M. Levi, brilliant mathematician, killed by an earthquake in Himalaya; Christopher Wordsworth, my close friend, who died in India; Cyril Clague, later H. M. Inspector; W. W. Greg, the great Elizabethan scholar; F. Dobson, later Professor of Greek at Bristol; A. Wedgwood, engineer, adventurer and novelist, died in S. America; and George Macauley Trevelyan, later the Master of the College.

In Spring 1901, I climbed again with my brother Hilton, still in residence. In the same year we made the

Official Tour and Report.

In January 1902, when I was taking my M. A. degree, I did some good new climbs in I Court, with Mackay and Dobson.

In the autumn of 1901, the Vice-Master, Aldis Wright, declared that the college must take cognisance of roof-climbing, and decide whether or not it should be declared illegal. The Council appointed two of the junior Fellows, George Trevelyan and Gilbert Walker (later Sir Gilbert, the Indian Hydrographer Royal, and member of the A. C.) to report; with power to co-opt *me*, as a non-resident member of Committee. We went up and did the climbs and circuits in full daylight, with two of our former enemies, the College Porters, carrying the fire-ropes behind us through the Courts, in procession! As the result of the Official Report, the practice was made (officially) illegal.

After the First War, about 1920, a very clever Guide was written to the St John's roofs, which closely copied my 'parodied-Alpine' style. It was done by two 'Blues' – one of them Hartley, the great rowing blue.

A second edition of my Trinity Guide was produced,

early in the 30s I think; by a young Hurst, son of Sir Cecil, Legal advisor to the F.O. A horrible hotch-potch, that I stopped by wire and then allowed to go on, at his tearful pleading. Thank goodness, it is now out of print and, I hope, forgotten. It was execrable.

G.W.Y. 1948